The Haunting That Helped

Written and illustrated
by Rachel Forbes

Northkind Press
Sheffield, United Kingdom
www.northkindpress.co.uk

First published in 2026 by Northkind Press.

ISBN: 978-1-0676718-0-8

Printed and bound in United Kingdom

For Ralph, my chief story tester,
who always notices the magic.

In a really old town, there's a really old school. It doesn't look much, but it's actually quite cool.

There's something about it that nobody knows...it's really quite special, so stay on your toes.
SCHOOL

The
Headteacher's
mind was filled
with worry.
Repair bills kept
coming, and
there was no
spare money.

"I must find a
way to make
money soon.
Without some
repairs, our
school will be
doomed..."

The roof
needed fixing.
The windows
did too.

The heating
made noises
you'd hear
at the Zoo...

Sometimes
the books
even
flew
off the
shelves...

..and doors opened
wide, all by
themselves.....

The school was sturdy, its bricks old and strong.
But he couldn't afford to fix what was wrong.

The Headteacher didn't realise he wasn't in this alone, or that two ghostly children called the school home. Don't be afraid as you step inside, you could find new friends appear by your side.

Percy is four and Evie is six.
Grown-ups can't see them; with kids it's a mix.
Some have the sight, though it's rarely believed -
they're the "easily distracted" ones people misread.

The teachers all say, "It's nonsense, don't fret -
just squeaky old floors and a draught, I'd bet."
But chairs scrape and shuffle with no one in sight...
and strange things keep happening night after night.

Evie loves scares, Percy loves tricks...
there's laughter and mayhem, and muddles to fix.
They hide surprises here and there, their favourite is
glitter - it gets everywhere!

They love to leave their clues behind
for sharp-eyed children keen to find.
Then off they drift, both pleased and proud,
and giggle somewhere not too loud.

Ssshhhh… did you hear that giggling sound?
Percy and Evie must be around.

A row of socks on
classroom hooks...

...some googly eyes on
library books.

A toy giraffe
upon the
stairs...

...some knotted ribbons on
the chairs.

Some toy cars
parked along a
shelf...

...a coat peg
wearing one
lone belt.

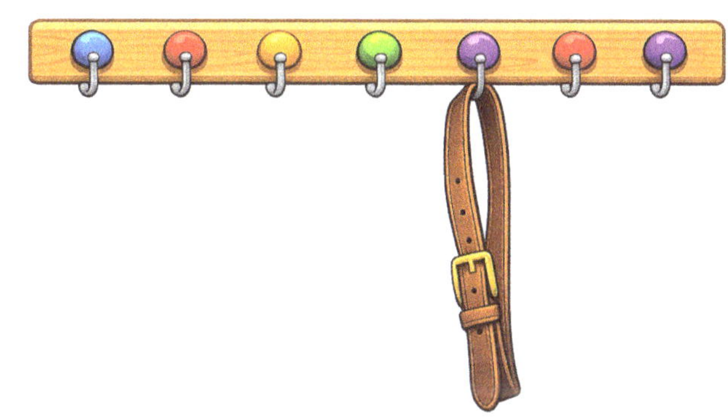

Ssshhhh... did you
hear that
giggling sound?
Percy and Evie
must be around.

When they heard that their school was in serious
trouble, our two friendly ghosts got themselves all in
a muddle.

Evie was frozen, her mind full of fear.
Percy was excited - he'd had an idea!

Evie listened with patience - that's what good friends
do - but she drew the line fast when he mentioned
POO!

POO PRANK TOY!

MAKE POO WHERE THERE SHOULDN'T BE POO!

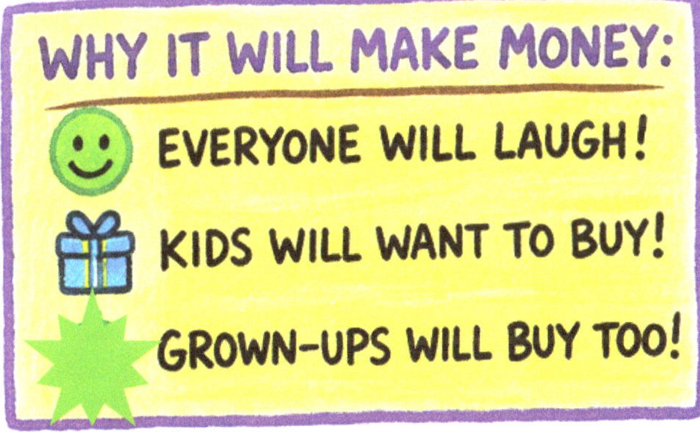

They needed help, this was too big for two, so they gathered all of the friends that they knew. In the playground together, they formed a team, to build a bold and brilliant scheme.

The ideas flowed so fast and free, like leaves blown from a giant tree. A game, a sign, a song, a stall, and one good plan to unite them all.

Out came paints and paper too, plus crayons in yellow, green, and blue. They all made posters, big and bright - some a bit wonky - all just right.

They painted a banner with swishes and flair. They got splodges on noses and drips in their hair!

By morning, drifting
through the air,
came shining posters
for a fair.

Matching leaflets
fluttered down,
through every
letterbox in town.

They twirled like
leaves, then settled
neat by every door -
no mean feat!

A week later, the playground buzzed with sound, as
families and children gathered around.

Stalls filled the space, a colourful treat.
There was music and laughter and running feet.

BOO

Though no one could see them, the ghosts
helped all day, and this meant that mischief
wasn't too far away. Your ball might stray,
your cap might fly. There's no wind at all, so
you might wonder why...
Ssshhhh... did you hear that giggling sound?
Percy and Evie must be around.

When the fair was over and the crowds had gone,
the headteacher counted the coins one-by-one.
"Our school is saved!", he said, his voice clear
and loud, "I don't know who did it, but I'm
incredibly proud!"

The ghosts and their friends
were filled with glee! As
pleased as they could possibly
be. Swelling with pride, they
danced with delight,
knowing their plan had
worked out just right.

And if you visit this school someday,
Percy and Evie might want you to play.
If you believe in them, you might just see…

…two new friends waiting patiently.

Glitter might swirl,
toy cars might meet.
Adults should
keep an eye on their
feet.

Percy has been known
to tie laces together.
Like that unfortunate
time with the
OFSTED
inspector.....

Sssssshhhh... did you hear that giggling sound?
Percy and Evie must still be around....

SCHOOL
The
End

At Northkind Press we know that everyone
has a story to tell.

Do you have an idea for a story?

We want to hear from you!

You might have an idea for Percy and Evie's
next adventure... or for a different story
altogether.

Contact office@northkindpress.co.uk or visit
www.northkindpress.co.uk